Go for The Code 2nd Edition

C

A primer for the Explode The Code series

Nancy Hall

EDUCATORS PUBLISHING SERVICE
Cambridge and Toronto

Cover art: Hugh Price

Mayfield, PA, in April 2015
ISBN 978-0-8388-7821-7

5 PAH 19

Color or mark the one that is different.

Trace the letter **c** with your finger. This letter has the sound you hear at the beginning of 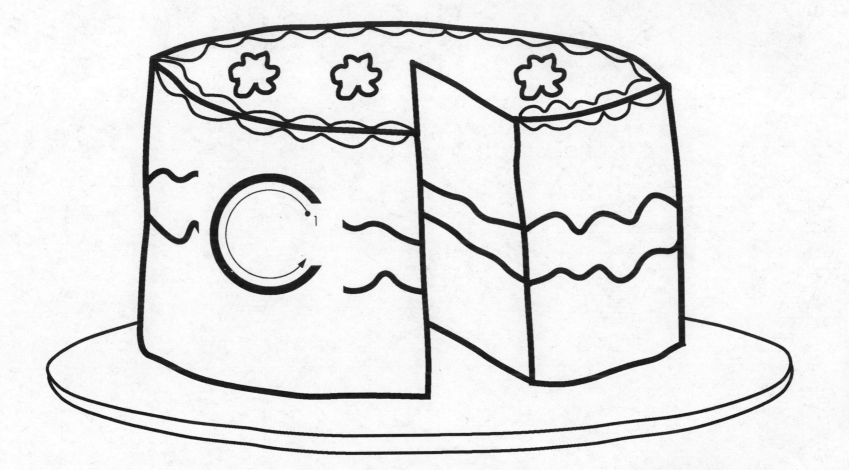. Say the sound.

Capital letters are used
to begin sentences and names.
A capital **c** looks like this: C.
Capital letters are two spaces tall.

Cc

Follow the lines from the **c** to the picture whose name begins with the /k/ sound.

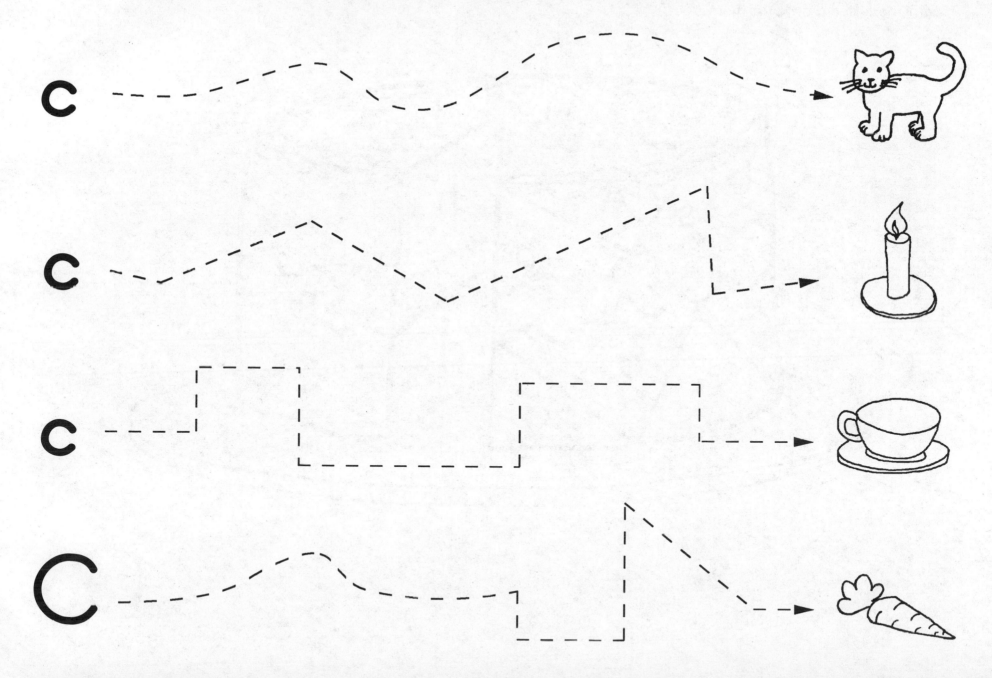

Say the name of the picture. Now say the sound that comes at the beginning of 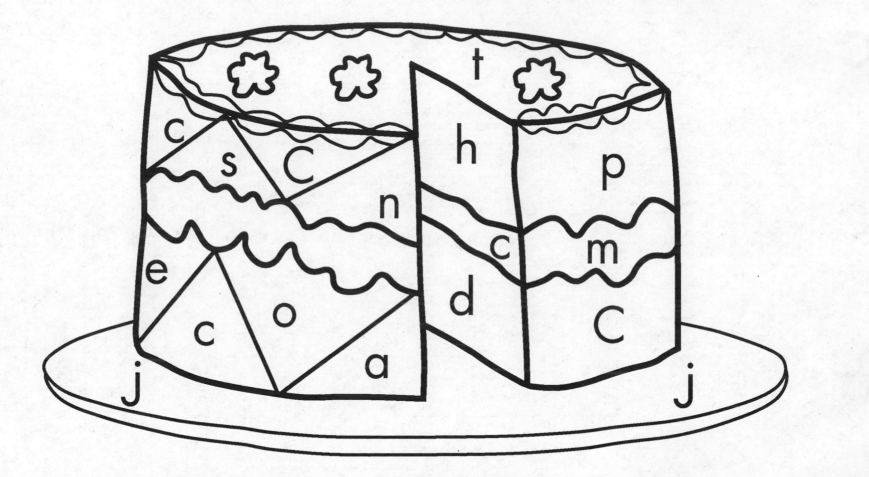. Color only the sections with the letter c or C in them.

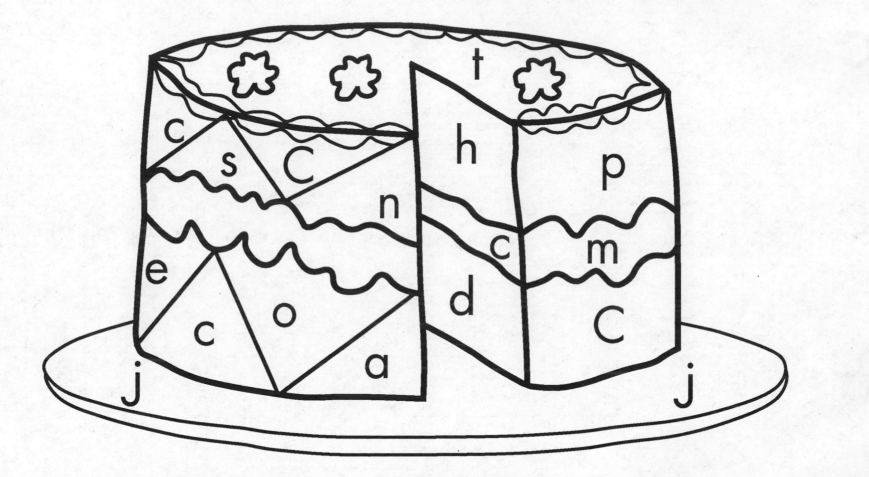

Cc

Look carefully at the letter in the box. Circle the letters that match it.

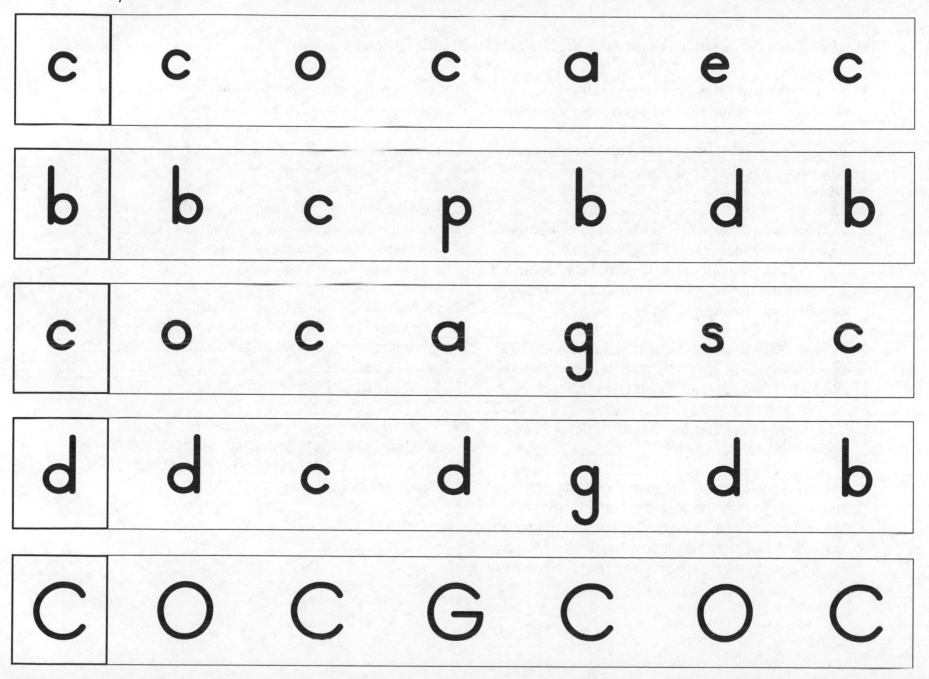

c	c	o	c	a	e	c
b	b	c	p	b	d	b
c	o	c	a	g	s	c
d	d	c	d	g	d	b
C	O	C	G	C	O	C

5

Teacher: Read the directions aloud while the students listen and work on page 7.

1. I am thinking of a dessert that is sweet and delicious. It is covered with frosting and sometimes we put candles on it. What is it? [cake] Put your finger on the **cake.** What sound do you hear at the beginning of **cake?** Color the **cake** any way you wish.

2. I am thinking of something that has to be lighted. Its flame glows and gives off light. What is it? [candle] Put your finger on the **candle.** What sound does **candle** begin with? Say the sound. Give the **candle** some smoke.

3. Find something on this page that you can use to make your hair neat. It is flat and has teeth. When you pull it through your hair, it takes the tangles out. What is it? [comb] Put your finger on the **comb.** What sound does **comb** begin with? Draw a circle around the **comb.**

4. I am thinking of an animal that makes the milk we drink. Can you say the sound this animal makes? What is this animal called? [cow] Put your finger on the **cow.** What sound does **cow** begin with? Say the sound again. Color the horns and spots on the **cow.**

5. I am thinking of a vegetable that is orange. You can eat it raw for a snack. Rabbits like to eat it, too. What is this vegetable called? [carrot] Put your finger on the **carrot.** What sound does **carrot** begin with? Color the **carrot** orange.

6. I am thinking of something you can drink from. Sometimes it sits on a saucer. What is it? [cup] Put your finger on the **cup.** Say the sound that **cup** begins with. Draw a box around the **cup.**

7. I am thinking of something that you ride in. It has four wheels and a motor, and needs gas to run. What is it? [car] Put your finger on the **car.** What sound does **car** begin with? Say the sound again. Draw a road for the **car** to drive on.

8. That last picture is of a lovable animal. It is soft and furry and says meow. What is it? [cat] Put your finger on the **cat.** What sound does **cat** begin with? Carefully color the **cat.**

Listen; then follow the directions.

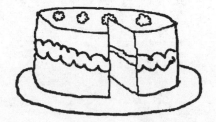

Draw a line from the box to each picture whose name begins with the sound /k/ as in .

C

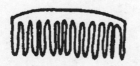

Follow the arrows to write the letter **c**, which says /k/as in 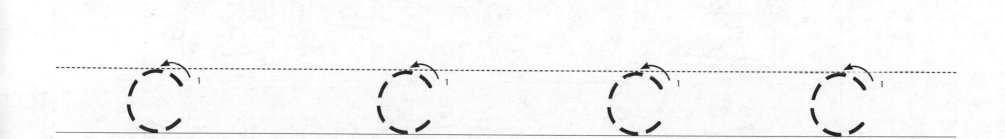 . Say the sound aloud.

Notice that **c** is only one space tall. Trace the letters.

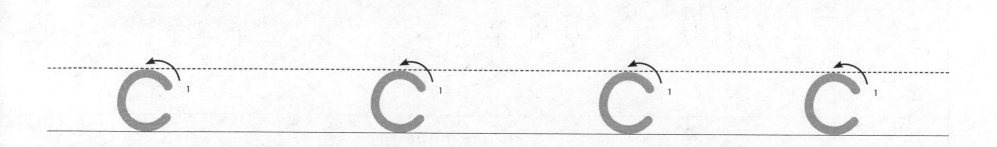

c usually says /k/ as in . On each line color the picture whose name begins with the sound /k/.

Trace the letters.

C   C   C   C   C

Copy the letter.

C

◯ each picture whose name begins with **c**. Write **c** below those pictures.

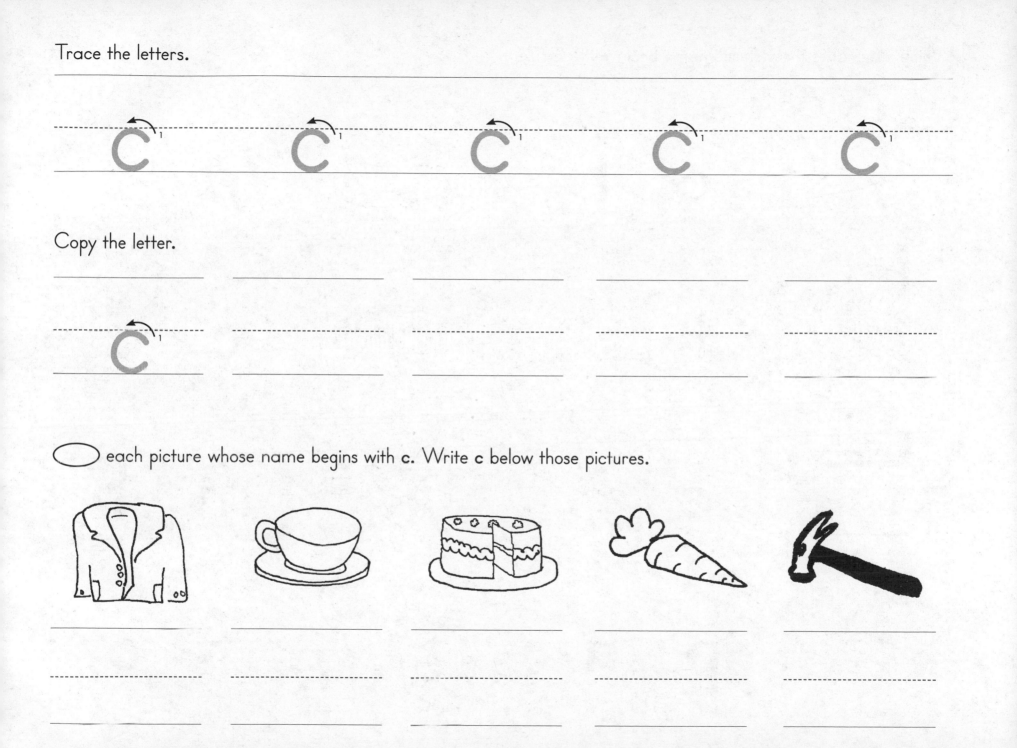

Which letter does the picture's name begin with? Circle it.

c   t   d   c

t   r   c   d

c   t   m   b

p   h   f   c

12

Say the name of the picture and the sound of its first letter.	Find the letter. Circle it.	Write the letter.
	d f c s	
	p c j r	
	b n t s	
	t c m p	
	j r s c	

Which sound does the word begin with? Write the letter that stands for the sound.

_____

_____

_____

_____

- - - - - - - - - - - - -

- - - - - - - - - - - - -

- - - - - - - - - - - - -

- - - - - - - - - - - - -

_____

_____

_____

_____

_____

_____

_____

_____

- - - - - - - - - - - - -

- - - - - - - - - - - - -

- - - - - - - - - - - - -

- - - - - - - - - - - - -

_____

_____

_____

_____

Color or mark the one that is different.

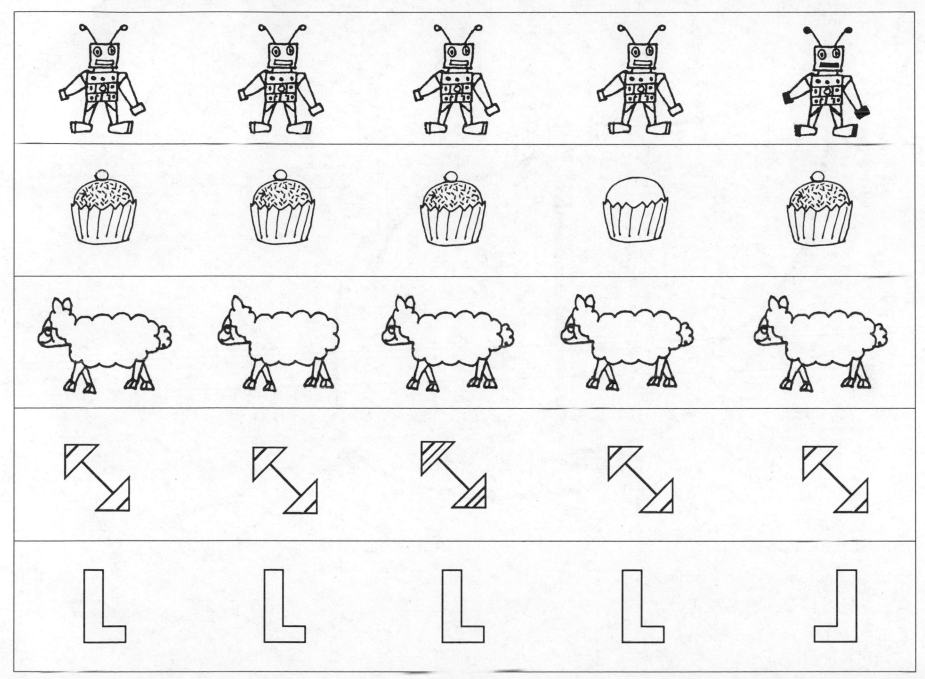

Trace the letter l with your finger. This letter has the sound you hear at the beginning of 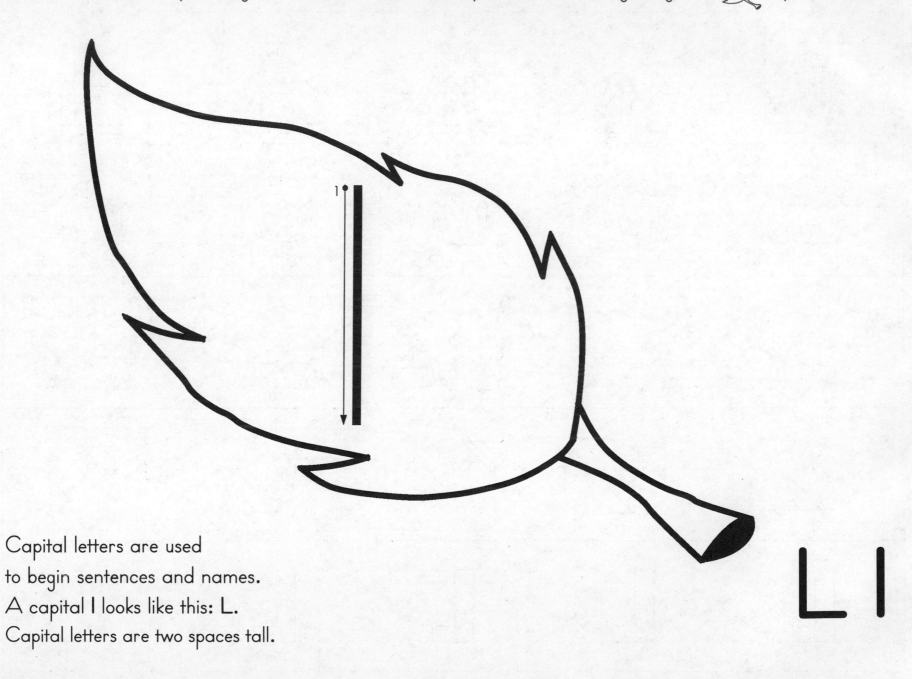. Say the sound.

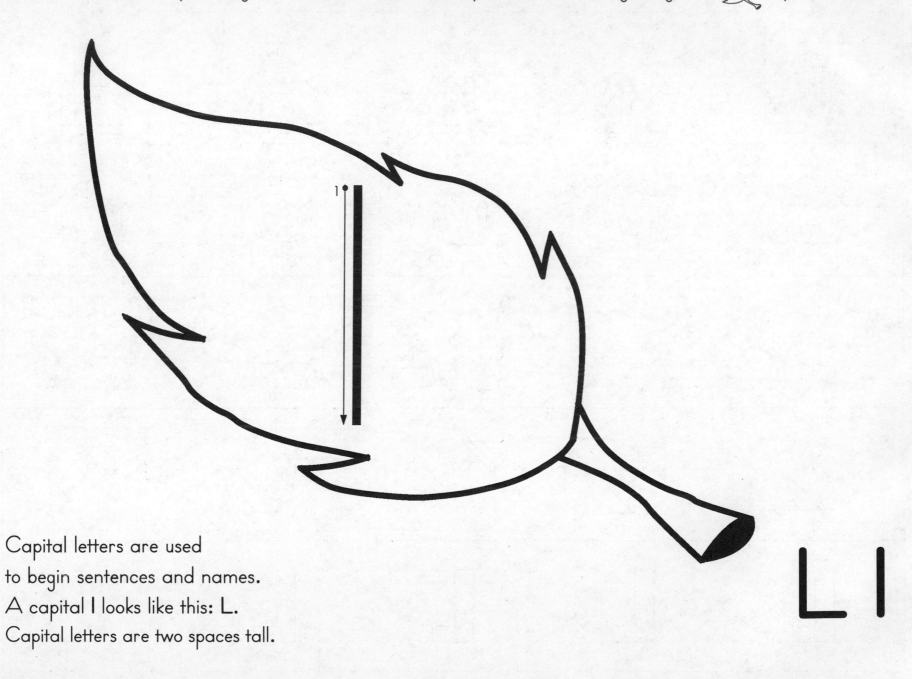

Capital letters are used
to begin sentences and names.
A capital l looks like this: L.
Capital letters are two spaces tall.

L l

Follow the lines from the l to the picture whose name begins with the /l/ sound.

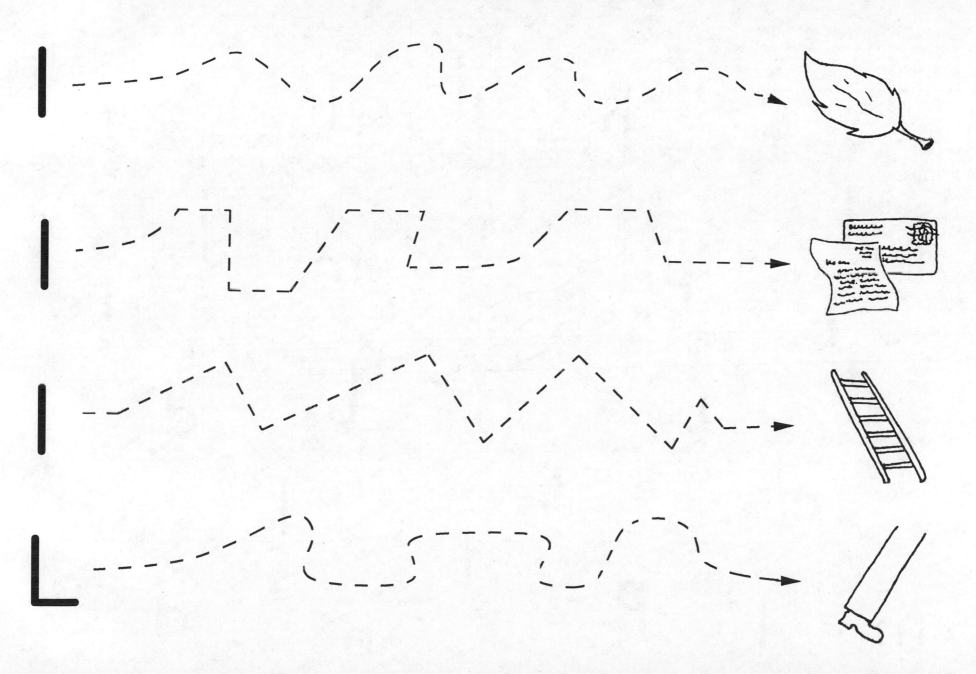

Draw a line from the leaf to each letter that begins its name. Can you find seven letters?

Look carefully at the letter in the box. Circle the letters that match it.

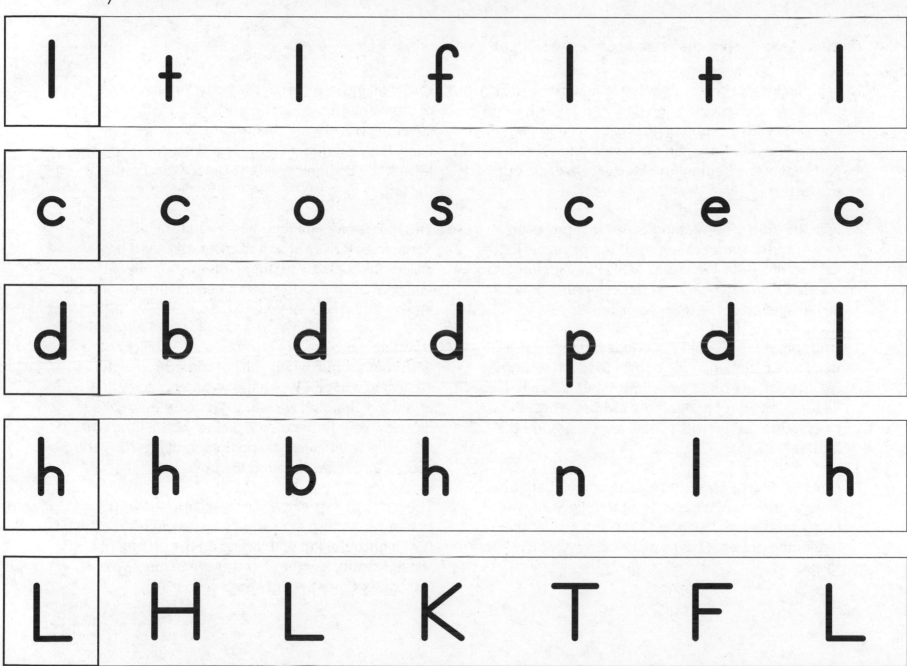

| l | t | l | f | l | t | l |

| c | c | o | s | c | e | c |

| d | b | d | d | p | d | l |

| h | h | b | h | n | l | h |

| L | H | L | K | T | F | L |

Teacher: Read the directions aloud while the students listen and work on page 21.

1. I am thinking of something that is sent in the mail. A person writes a message on paper and puts it in an envelope with a stamp on it. What am I thinking of? [letter] Put your finger on the **letter**. What sound do you hear at the beginning of **letter?** Draw an X on the **letter.**

2. I am thinking of something green that grows on a tree or bush. Sometimes it turns red or yellow in the fall and drops off. What is it? [leaf] Put your finger on the **leaf**. Can you hear /l/ at the beginning of **leaf?** Say /l/, and color the **leaf** green, red, or yellow.

3. Find something on this page that you might use to climb up high in a tree or on a roof. It has rungs to put your feet on as you climb. What is it called? [ladder] Put your finger on the **ladder**. What sound does **ladder** begin with? Draw a circle around the **ladder.**

4. I am thinking of a very large wild animal that has a mane and roars. What is its name? [lion] Put your finger on the **lion**. Say the sound you hear at the beginning of **lion**. Draw a piece of meat for the **lion** to eat.

5. I am thinking of a part of the body. You have two of them and they help you walk. You wear pants to cover them and keep them warm. What are they? [legs] Put your finger on the **leg**. What sound do you hear at the beginning of **leg?** Draw a box around the **leg.**

6. This object gives off light when you turn it on. Sometimes it has a shade to cover it. What is it called? [lamp] Put your finger on the picture of the **lamp**. What sound does **lamp** begin with? Color the **lamp**shade any color you wish.

7. Now find a picture of a part of a face. You lick these with your tongue when you eat something tasty. They help you talk. When the weather is cold, they might get chapped and sting. What are they called? [lips] Put your finger on the picture of the **lips**. What sound do you hear at the beginning of **lips?** Say the sound. Draw a face around the **lips.**

8. The last picture is of the part of a lamp that gives off light. You can turn it on and off by a switch. What is it? [lightbulb] Put your finger on the picture of the **lightbulb**. Say the sound at the beginning of **lightbulb**. Color the **lightbulb** yellow.

Listen; then follow the directions.

21

Draw a line from the tag to each picture whose name begins with /l/ as in .

 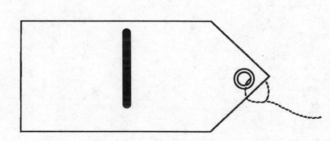 

Follow the arrows to write the letter l, which says /l/ as in 🍃. Say the sound aloud.

Notice that l is two spaces tall. Trace the letters.

Which letter does the picture's name begin with? Circle it.

| l p | t l | k f | l h |
| l d | s c | l m | c l |

Trace the letters.

Copy the letter.

◯ each picture whose name begins with l. Write l below those pictures.

25

Draw a line from each picture to the letter that begins its name.

d c l t c l f c d

Say the name of the picture and the sound of its first letter.	Find the letter. Circle it.	Write the letter.
	p l f m	
	l t n c	
	r l h m	
	l c d p	
	d j f l	

Which sound does the word begin with? Write the letter that stands for the sound.

_____
- - - - - - - - - -
_____

_____
- - - - - - - - - -
_____

_____
- - - - - - - - - -
_____

_____
- - - - - - - - - -
_____

_____
- - - - - - - - - -
_____

_____
- - - - - - - - - -
_____

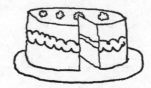

_____
- - - - - - - - - -
_____

_____
- - - - - - - - - -
_____

Color or mark the one that is different.

Trace the letter **g** with your finger. This letter has the sound you hear at the beginning of . Say the sound.

Capital letters are used
to begin sentences and names.
A capital **g** looks like this: G.
Capital letters are two spaces tall.

Gg

Follow the lines from the **g** to the picture whose name begins with the /g/ sound.

g

g

g

G

Draw a line from the goat to each letter that begins its name. Can you find seven letters?

g d h g d

t f c j

s l

g

n d p

b r

g d f

p g

j g

c c

Look carefully at the letter in the box. Circle the letters that match it.

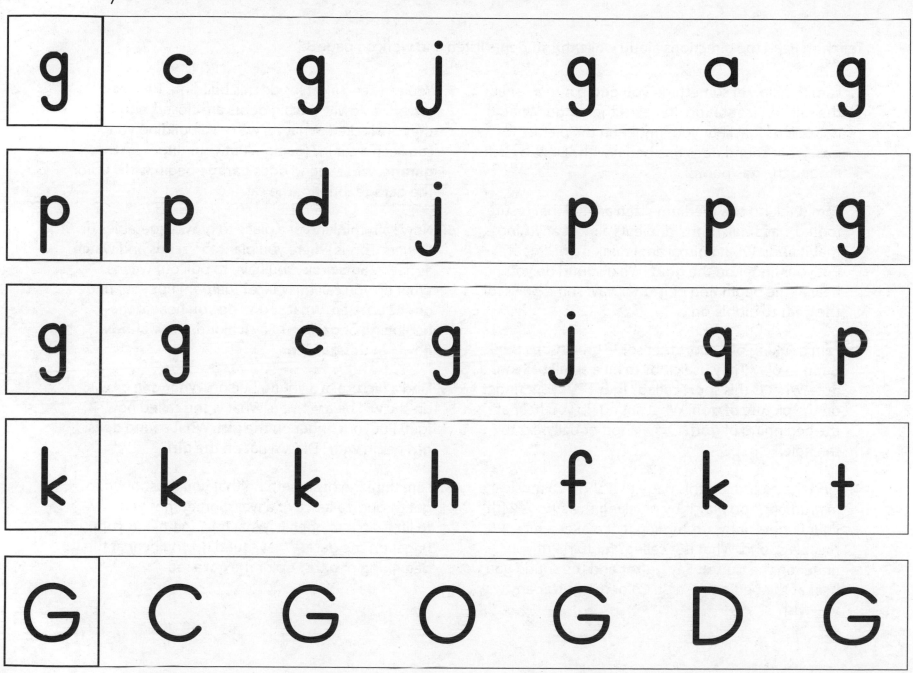

| g | c | g | j | g | a | g |

| p | p | d | j | p | p | g |

| g | g | c | g | j | g | p |

| k | k | k | h | f | k | t |

| G | C | G | O | G | D | G |

33

Teacher: Read the directions aloud while the students listen and work on page 35.

1. I am thinking of something you pump into a car at the self-service station. It makes the car go. What is it called? [gas] Put your finger on the picture for **gas.** What sound does **gas** begin with? Draw a circle around the **gas** pump.

2. I am thinking of a medium-sized animal that is sure-footed, has small horns, and eats almost anything that it finds. What animal am I thinking of? [goat] Put your finger on the **goat.** What sound do you hear at the beginning of **goat?** Draw some grass for the **goat** to nibble on.

3. I am thinking of a sport that some grown-ups think is fun to play. They use clubs to hit a small ball into a hole. What is this sport called? [golf] Put your finger on the picture of **golf.** What sound do you hear at the beginning of **golf?** Draw another ball next to the hole.

4. Find the picture on this page that shows a musical instrument. You play it by plucking the strings with your fingers or by strumming it. It makes a nice, mellow sound. What is it called? [guitar] Put your finger on the **guitar.** Say **guitar** and the sound you hear at the beginning of it. Color the **guitar** any way you wish.

5. You can keep a car inside this building. The car is driven in slowly, the big doors are closed, and then they are locked. What do we call a building you can keep a car in? [garage] Put your finger on the **garage.** What sound does **garage** begin with? Color the **garage,** but not the car.

6. Now I am thinking of a place to grow vegetables or flowers. This is where you plant the seeds and watch as new plants grow. You have to pull out weeds. What do you call this place? [garden] Put your finger on the **garden.** What sound do you hear at the beginning of **garden?** Say it aloud. Draw another flower in this **garden.**

7. Find a picture of a young person. When she grows up she will be a woman. What is she called now? [girl] Put your finger on the **girl.** What sound does **girl** begin with? Draw a hat on the **girl.**

8. I am thinking of something that you must open to get through a fence or a wall. Sometimes you have to lift a latch to open it. What is it? [gate] Put your finger on the **gate.** What sound do you hear at the beginning of **gate?** Color the **gate** red.

Listen; then follow the directions.

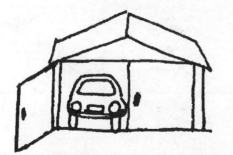

Say the sound of each letter. Then color the picture whose name begins with that sound.

Follow the arrows to write the letter **g**, which says /g/ as in 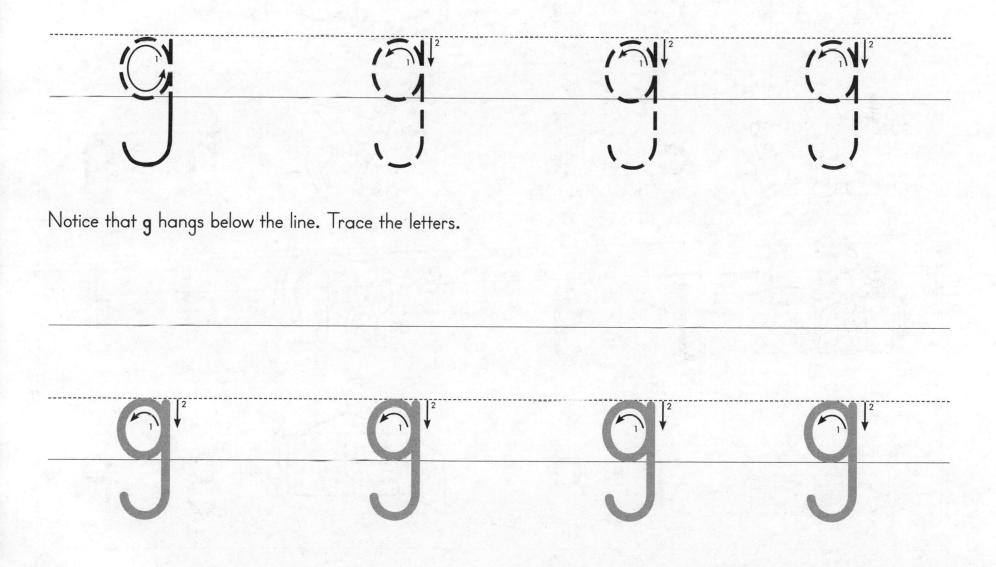. Say the sound aloud.

Notice that **g** hangs below the line. Trace the letters.

Which letter does the picture's name begin with? Circle it.

l   g   c   d

c   l   h   g

j   g   d   g

g   c   g   p

Trace the letters.

g g g g g

Copy the letter.

g

⬭ each picture whose name begins with **g**. Write **g** below those pictures.

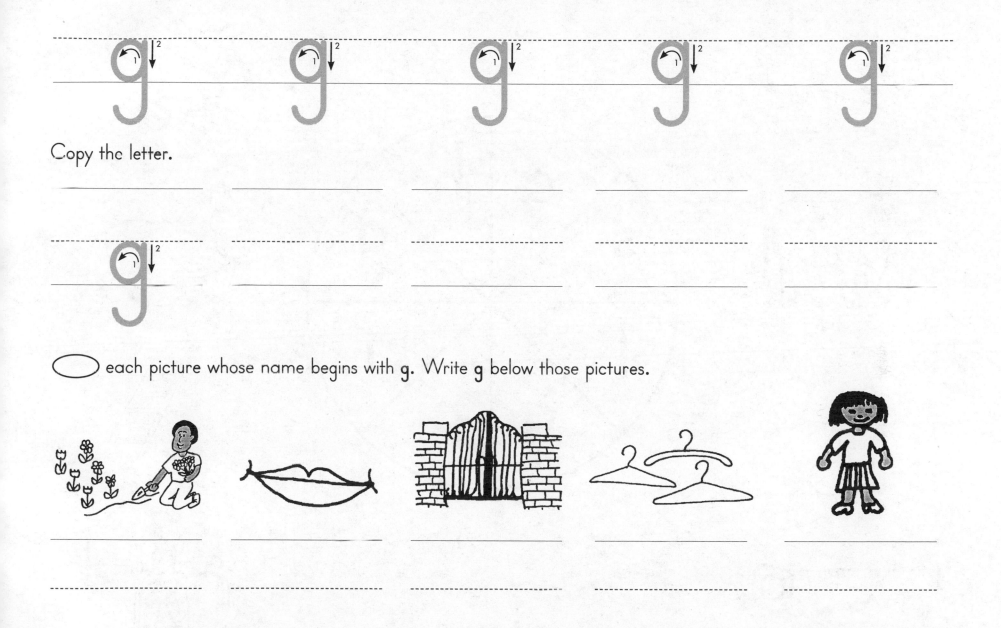

Draw a line from the picture to the letter that begins its name.

s c h g l g c l

Say the name of the picture and the sound of its first letter.	Find the letter. Circle it.	Write the letter.
	c g k	
	r s c	
	g n j	
	m l p	
	f b h	

41

Which sound does the word begin with? Write the letter that stands for the sound.

Color or mark the one that is different.

Trace the letter **w** with your finger. This letter has the sound you hear at the beginning of . Say the sound.

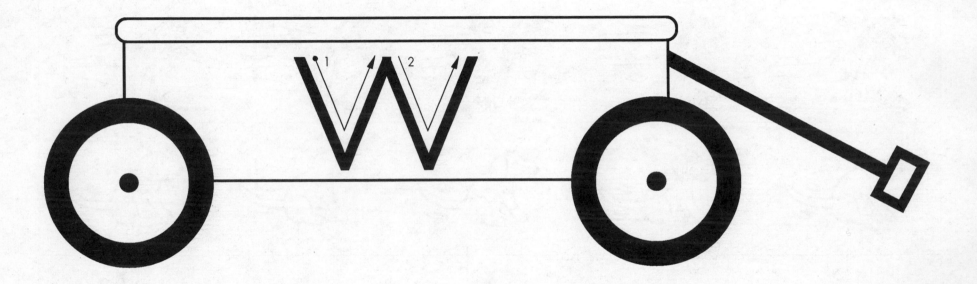

Capital letters are used
to begin sentences and names.
A capital **w** looks like this: W.
Capital letters are two spaces tall.

Ww

Draw a line from each  to each letter that begins its name. Can you find seven letters?

w l   t

g d   p

    g   l

m m

    n   w

    w m w h m n

h c   n w

    w

    p n j p w

45

Teacher: Read the directions aloud while the students listen and work on page 47.

1. I am thinking of something you wear on your wrist so you know the time. What is it? [watch] Put your finger on the **watch.** What sound does **watch** begin with? Draw a box around the **watch.**

2. This is something you can do with your eyes. When you flick one eyelid closed, it is called a _____ [wink]. Put your finger on the picture of the person **winking.** What sound do you hear at the beginning of **wink**? Draw a hat on the head of the person who is **winking.**

3. I am thinking of something that has four wheels and a long handle. You can haul things in it when you pull it behind you. What is it? [wagon] Put your finger on the **wagon.** What sound does **wagon** begin with? Color the **wagon** red.

4. I am thinking of something spiders spin. It helps them catch insects for food. What is it? [web] Put your finger on the **web.** What sound does **web** begin with? Draw a circle around the **web.**

5. The apple has something in it. What is it? [worm] Put your finger on the **worm.** You wouldn't want to eat the **worm.** What sound does **worm** begin with? Color the **worm.**

6. I am thinking of something that you throw waste paper into. There is at least one of these in every classroom. You dump the pencil sharpener dust into it and throw old papers in it when you clean out your desk. What is it? [wastebasket] Put your finger on the **wastebasket.** What sound does **wastebasket** begin with? Draw an X on the **wastebasket.**

7. The last picture shows a machine that works when the wind blows. It can pump water. What is it called? [windmill] Put your finger on the **windmill.** What sound does **windmill** begin with? Carefully color the **windmill** any way you like.

Listen; then follow the directions.

Draw a line from the box to each picture whose name begins with /w/ as in 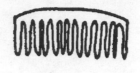 .

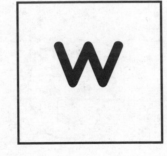

48

Follow the arrows to write the letter **w**, which says /w/ as in ⬚. Say the sound aloud.

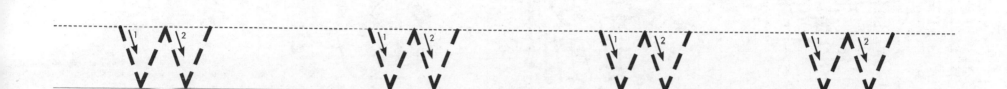

Notice that **w** is only one space tall. Trace the letters.

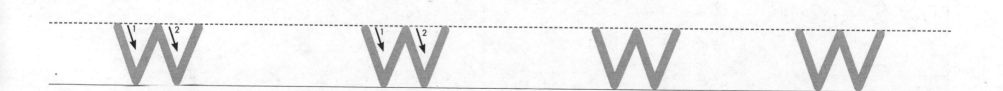

Which letter does the picture's name begin with? Circle it.

t l

w c

w m

b d

w n

h g

w g

d g

Trace the letters.

W   W   W   W   W

Copy the letter.

W

◯ each picture whose name begins with **w**. Write **w** below those pictures.

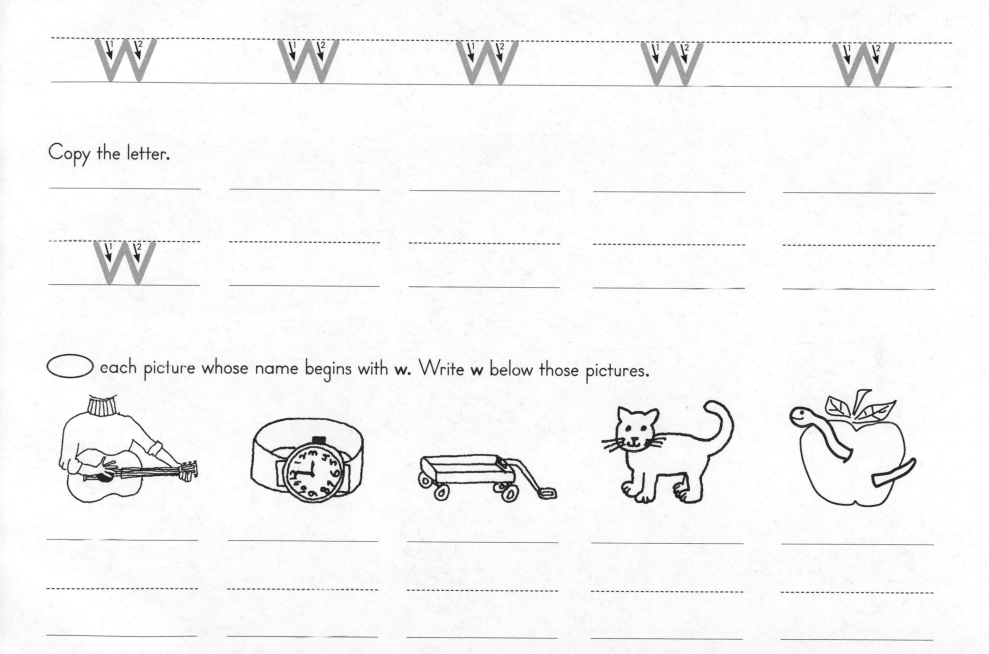

Which sound does the word begin with? Write the letter that stands for the sound.

Trace the letter **y** with your finger. This letter has the sound you hear at the beginning of . Say the sound.

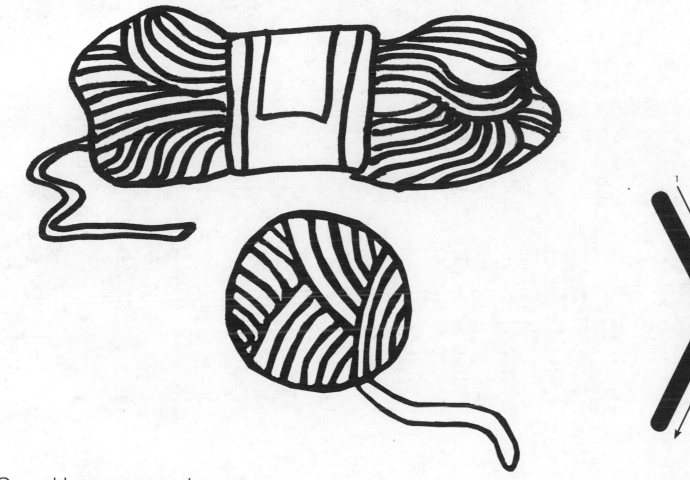

Capital letters are used
to begin sentences and names.
A capital y looks like this: Y.
Capital letters are two spaces tall.

Follow the lines from the y to the picture whose name begins with /y/.

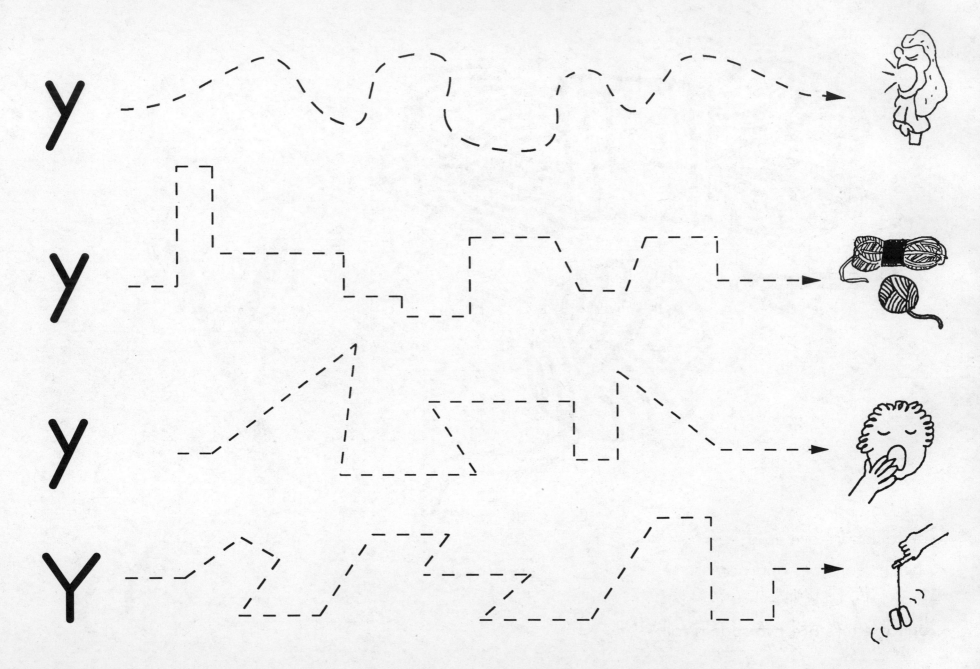

Draw a line from the yarn to each letter that begins its name. Can you find seven letters?

g

n

g

h

y

y

r

c

y

w

h

f

j

j

h

g

j

j

g

k

d

j

p

y

y

c

w

p

y

Teacher: Read the directions aloud while the students listen and work on page 57.

1. I am thinking of something that you do when you are sleepy or bored. Your mouth opens wide and you _____ [yawn; Note: act this out]. Put your finger on the picture for **yawn.** What sound do you hear at the beginning of **yawn?** Draw a circle around the person who is **yawning.**

2. Sometimes when you want to get someone's attention, you do this with your voice. What word means the same as "shout loudly"? (It rhymes with *bell.*) [yell] Put your finger on the picture for **yell.** What sound does **yell** begin with? Draw an X on the picture of the person who is **yelling.**

3. I am thinking of a toy on a string. You put the string around your finger and make the round object move up and down. What is it? [yo-yo] Put your finger on the **yo-yo.** What sound do you hear at the beginning of **yo-yo?** Say the sound again. Color the **yo-yo** the color you like best.

4. The last picture shows something soft and very long. When people knit, they put this on the knitting needles and weave it back and forth. What is this material called? [yarn] Put your finger on the **yarn.** What sound does **yarn** begin with? Color the **yarn** the same color as a shirt or sweater you have.

Listen; then follow the directions.

Say the sound of each letter. Then color the picture whose name begins with that sound.

Follow the arrows to write the letter y, which says /y/as in 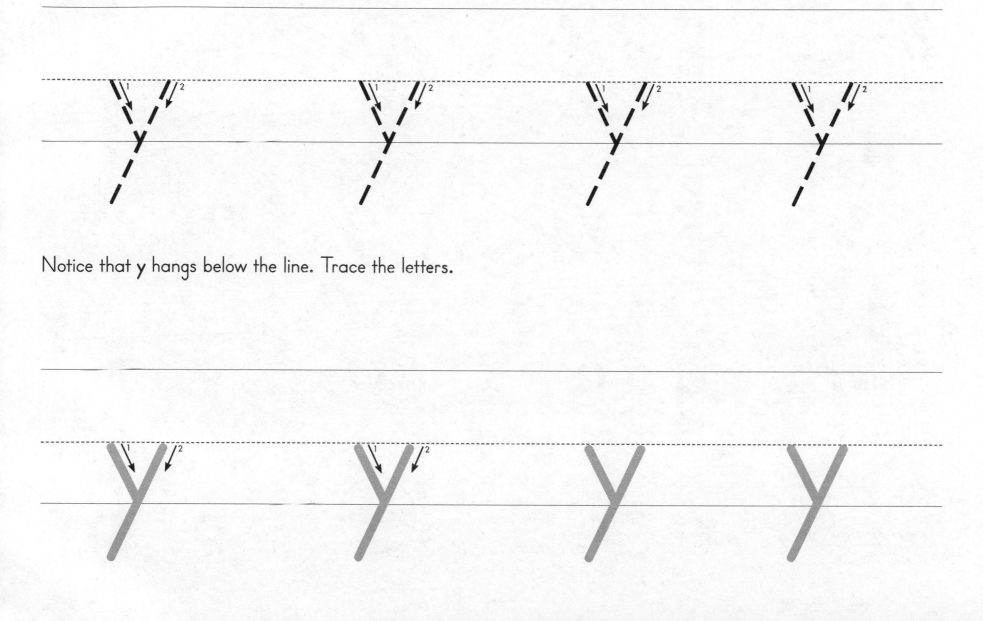. Say the sound aloud.

Notice that y hangs below the line. Trace the letters.

Which letter does the picture's name begin with? Circle it.

h   g   c   g

k   y   m   w

g   c   y   n

r   n   p   b

Trace the letters.

y   y   y   y   y

Copy the letter.

y

◯ each picture whose name begins with y. Write y below those pictures.

61

Which sound does the word begin with? Write the letter that stands for the sound.

Color or mark the one that is different.

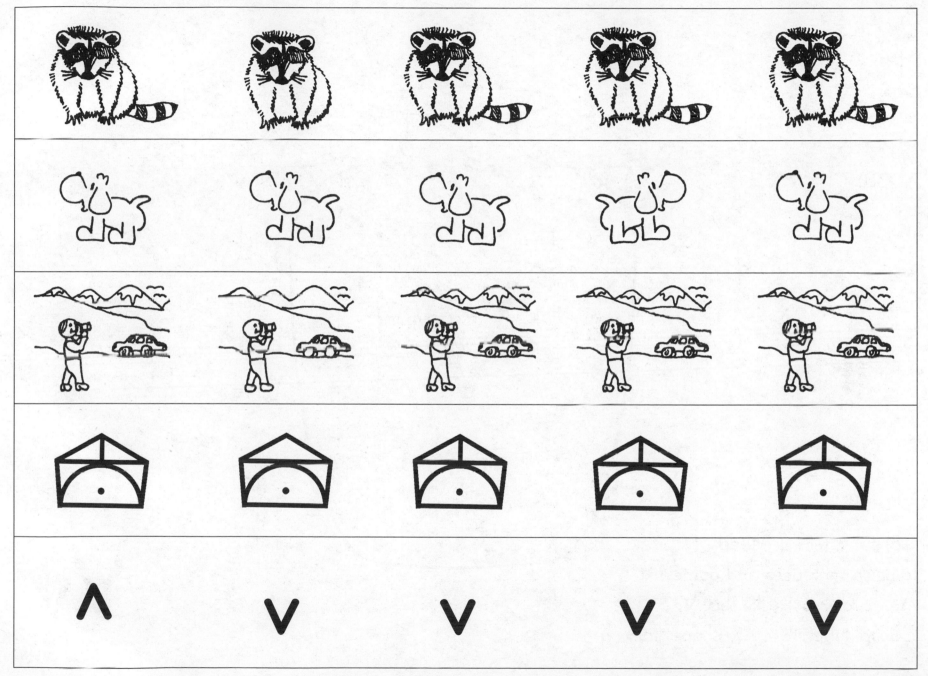

Trace the letter **v** with your finger. This letter has the sound you hear at the beginning of 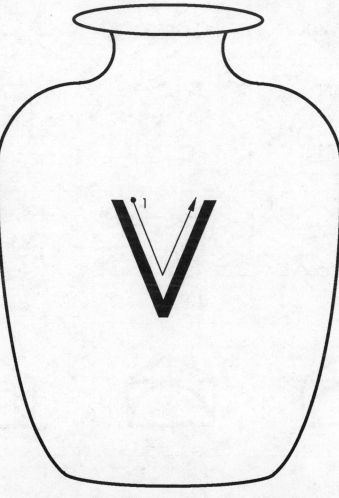. Say the sound.

Capital letters are used
to begin sentences and names.
A capital **v** looks like this: V.
Capital letters are two spaces tall.

Vv

Draw a line from each 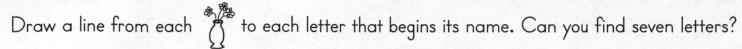 to each letter that begins its name. Can you find seven letters?

m

v

c

d

n

n

r

w

v

s

w

v

v

p

f

m

k   c

t   v

w

n

y

s

v

n

v

r

Teacher: Read the directions aloud while the students listen and work on page 67.

1. I am thinking of a greeting card with hearts and flowers on it. We send this kind of card to people we like on a special day in February. What do we call this card? [valentine] Put your finger on the **valentine.** What sound does **valentine** begin with? Carefully color the **valentine.**

2. I am thinking of a musical instrument you hold under your chin and play with a bow. It is made of wood. What is it called? [violin] Put your finger on the **violin.** Say the sound at the beginning of **violin.** Draw a circle around the **violin.**

3. I am thinking of something you put flowers in. Then you fill it with water. What is it? [vase] Put your finger on the **vase.** Say the sound at the beginning of **vase.** Color the **vase** blue.

4. This is a kind of clothing that has no sleeves. People wear it over a blouse or shirt. Find the picture of it. What is it called? [vest] Put your finger on the **vest.** What sound does **vest** begin with? Draw arms coming out of the **vest.**

5. I am thinking of a kind of plant. As it grows it climbs up the sides of buildings or trees. It has green leaves on it. Its name rhymes with *line*. What is it called? [vine] Put your finger on the **vine.** What sound does **vine** begin with? Draw a box around the **vines.**

6. The last picture shows some things that you might grow in a garden. They are good to eat and make you healthy. You can cook some of them, eat some of them raw, or put them in a salad. What are these things called? [vegetables] Put your finger on the **vegetables.** What sound does **vegetable** begin with? Color the **vegetables** green.

Listen; then follow the directions.

67

Which letter does the picture's name begin with? Circle it.

n v

k b

v r

v w

w g

v l

v y

n w

Trace the letters.

V   V   V   V   V

Copy the letter.

V

◯ each picture whose name begins with **v**. Write **v** below those pictures.

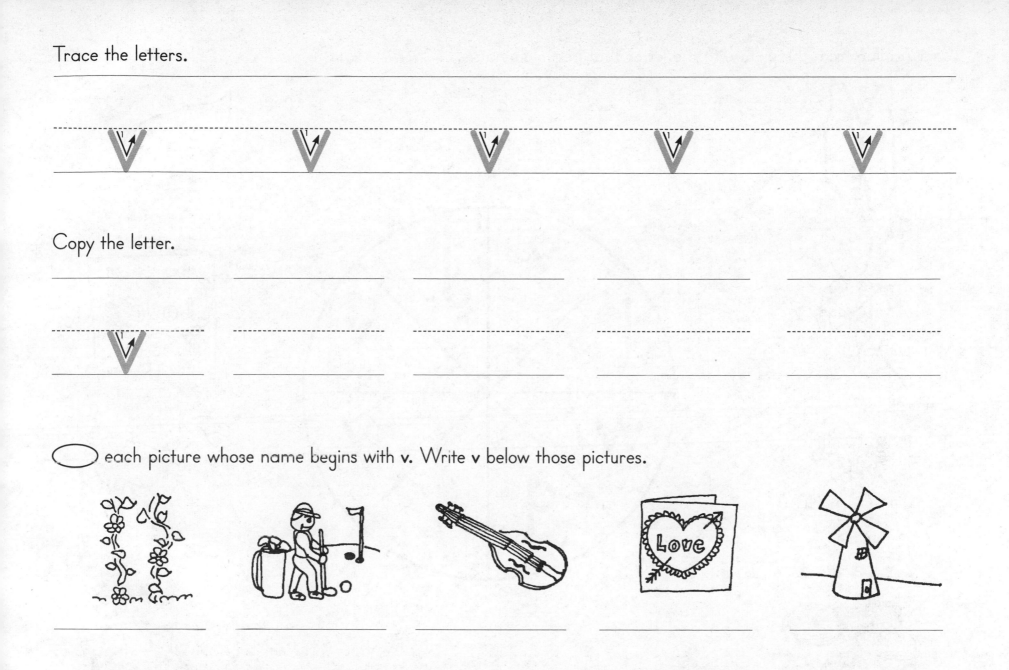

69

Draw a line from the picture to the letter that begins its name.

70

Say the name of the picture and the sound of its first letter.	Find the letter. Circle it.	Write the letter.
	v w j	
	p y k	
	y r v	
	v g l	
	c w b	

Which sound does the word begin with? Write the letter that stands for the sound.

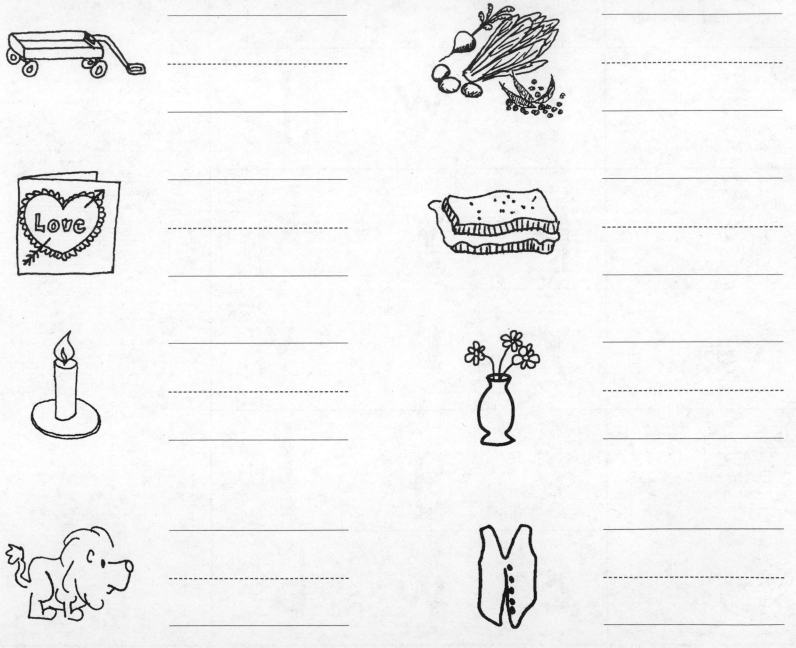

Trace the letter **z** with your finger. This letter has the sound you hear at the beginning of 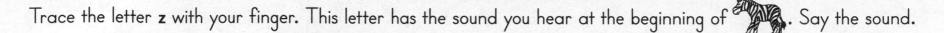. Say the sound.

Capital letters are used
to begin sentences and names.
A capital **z** looks like this: Z.
Capital letters are two spaces tall.

Zz

Draw a line from the zebra to each letter that begins its name. Can you find seven letters?

z v k z k n

v m w z l
w

z t n
k r

g w w y
c z

y n t z

y z p w r

Look carefully at the letter in the box. Circle the letters that match it.

z   w   z   m   y   n   z

w   w   m   v   w   w   k

g   g   y   g   d   p   g

Y   Y   K   W   Y   F   H

W   M   V   N   W   M   W

75

Teacher: Read the directions aloud while the students listen and work on page 77.

1. Find a picture of an animal that looks like a horse with black and white stripes. You might see one at a zoo. What is it? [zebra] Put your finger on the **zebra.** What sound does **zebra** begin with? Draw a circle around the **zebra.**

2. I am thinking of a design that goes back and forth across the page. It is called a **zigzag.** Put your finger on it. Say the sound at the beginning of **zigzag.** Draw another **zigzag** next to this one.

3. I am thinking of a place where wild animals are kept safely so that we can see them. What is this place called? [zoo] Put your finger on the **zoo.** Say the sound at the beginning of **zoo.** Draw a box around the **zoo.**

4. The last picture shows something that we use to close up or fasten clothing. It pulls along a little track. What is its name? [zipper] Put your finger on the **zipper.** What sound does **zipper** begin with? Draw a girl's head, arms, and legs in the dress with the **zipper.**

Listen; then follow the directions.

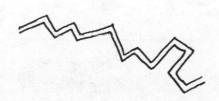

Say the sound of each letter. Then color the picture whose name begins with that sound.

Follow the arrows to write the letter **z**, which says /z/ as in 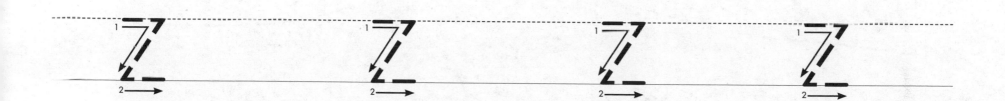. Say the sound aloud.

Notice that **z** is only one space tall. Trace the letters.

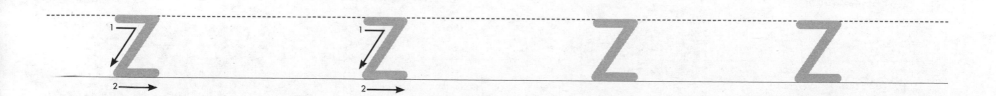

Draw a line from each picture to the letter that begins its name.

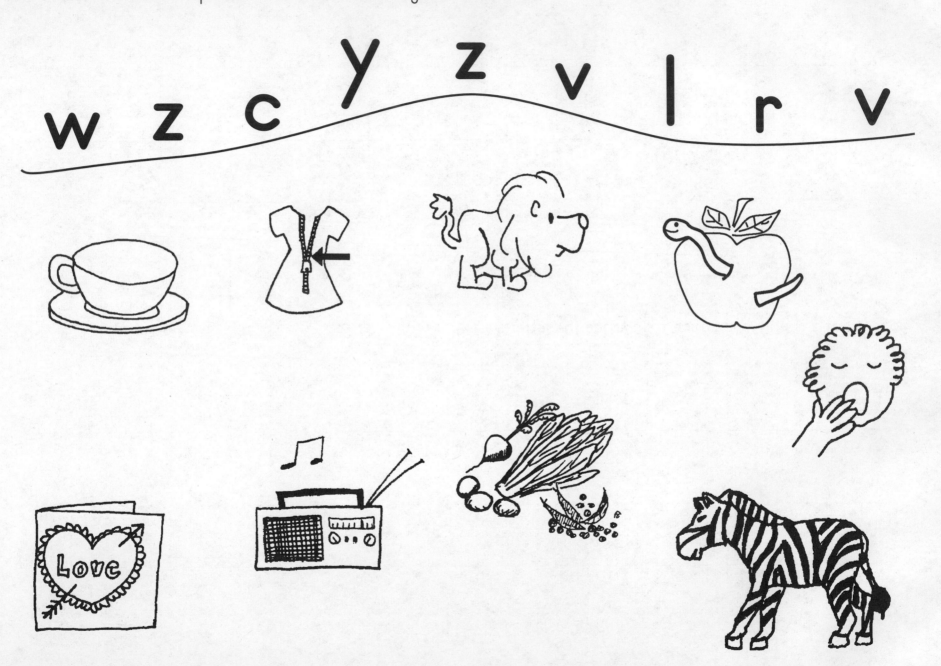

w z c y z v l r v

80

Trace the letters.

Z   Z   Z   Z   Z

Copy the letter.

Z

◯ each picture whose name begins with **z.** Write **z** below those pictures.

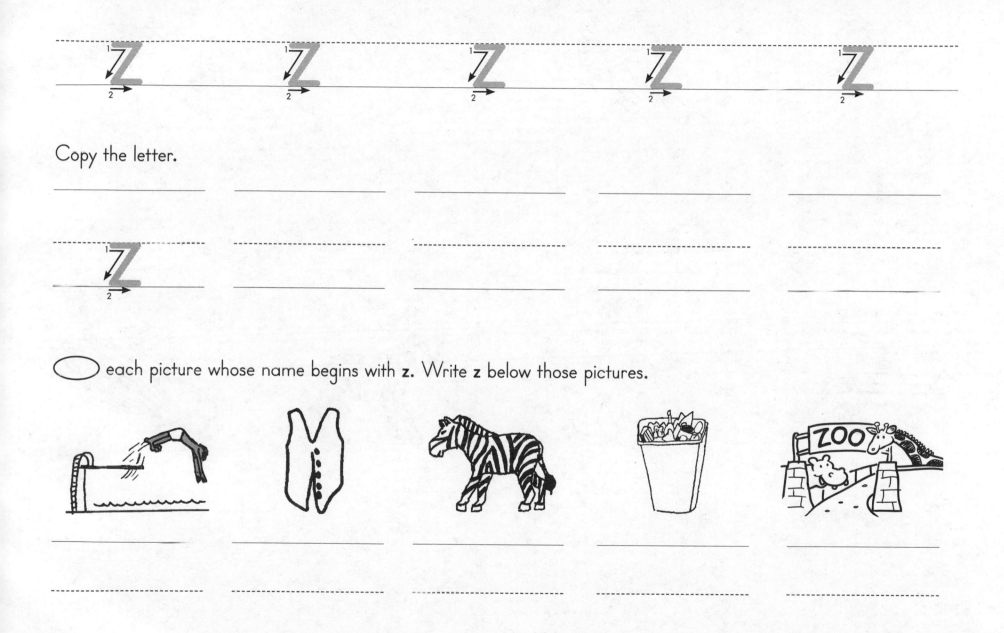

Which sound does the word begin with? Write the letter that stands for the sound.

- - - - - - - - - - - - -

- - - - - - - - - - - - -

- - - - - - - - - - - - -

- - - - - - - - - - - - -

- - - - - - - - - - - - -

- - - - - - - - - - - - -

- - - - - - - - - - - - -

- - - - - - - - - - - - -

Trace the letter **q** with your finger. This letter has the sound you hear at the beginning of **quilt** 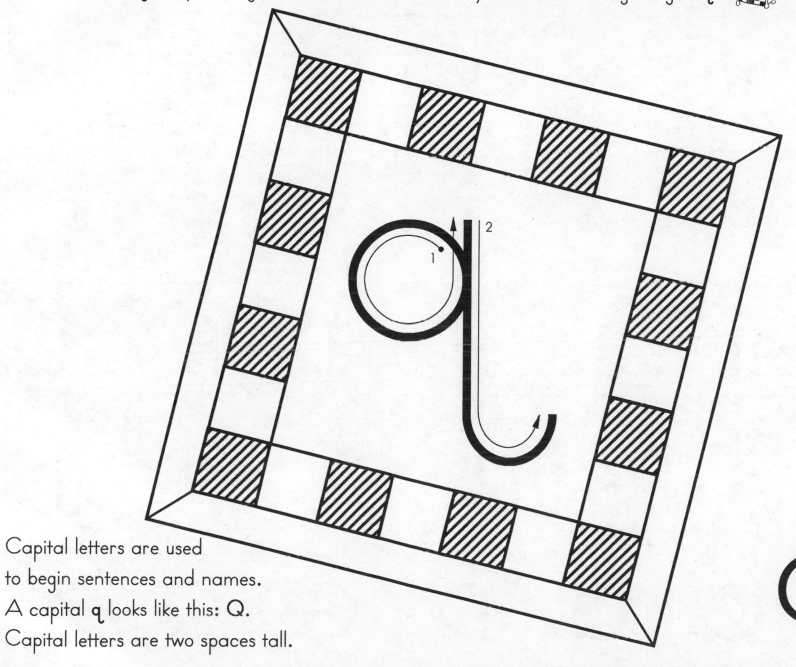. Say the sound.

Capital letters are used
to begin sentences and names.
A capital **q** looks like this: Q.
Capital letters are two spaces tall.

Qq

Look carefully at the letter in the box. Circle the letters that match it.

| w | m | w | v | w | m | w |

| z | z | v | z | v | z | r |

| q | q | g | g | q | p | q |

| g | g | p | j | q | d | g |

| Q | C | Q | D | G | Q | Z |

Follow the arrows to write the letter **q**, which says /**kw**/ as in 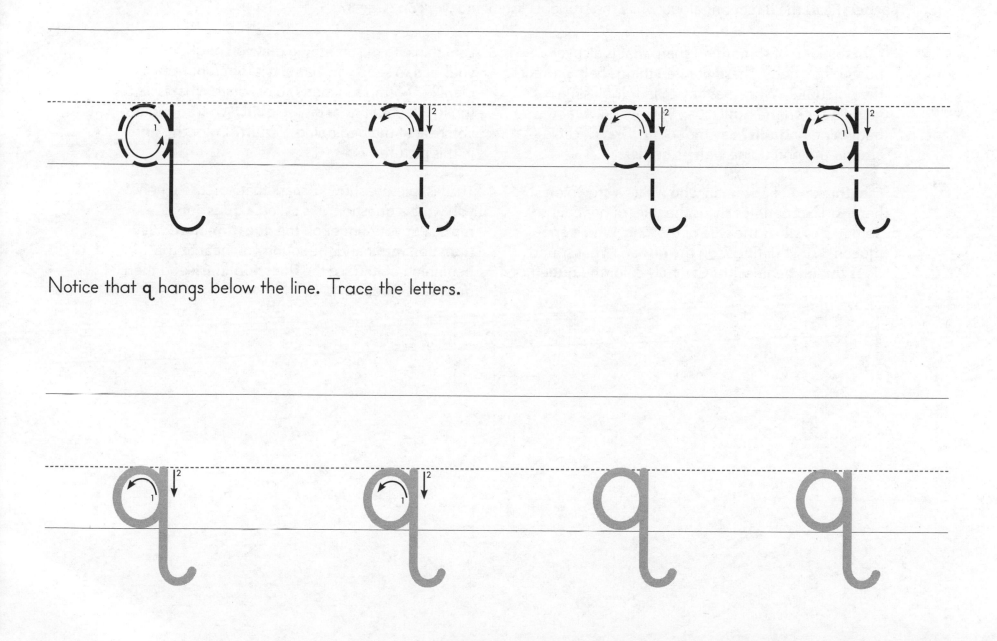. Say the sound aloud.

Notice that **q** hangs below the line. Trace the letters.

Teacher: Read the directions aloud while the students listen and work on page 87.

1. I am thinking of something sharp that is all over a porcupine's body. These pointed things help protect the porcupine. What are they called? [quills] Put your finger on the **quills.** Can you hear /kw/ at the beginning of **quills?** Say the sound. Draw a circle around the porcupine with its **quills.**

2. I am thinking of a woman who wears a crown on her head. Sometimes she is the ruler of her country. Sometimes she is the wife of the king. Who is she? [queen] Put your finger on the **queen.** What sound does **queen** begin with? Carefully color the **queen.**

3. I am thinking of something that you might put on your bed to keep you warm. It is different from a blanket. It often has many colors on it. What is it? [quilt] Put your finger on the **quilt.** What sound do you hear at the beginning of **quilt?** Color the **quilt** in this picture.

4. The last picture shows a mark that you use when you write a question. It is called a **question mark.** Put your finger on the **question mark.** Say **question mark** and the sound you hear at the beginning of it. Trace the **question mark** and then draw a box around it.

Listen; then follow the directions.

Draw a line from each picture to the letter that begins its name.

g   z   q   v   z   v   q   l   w

Trace the letters.

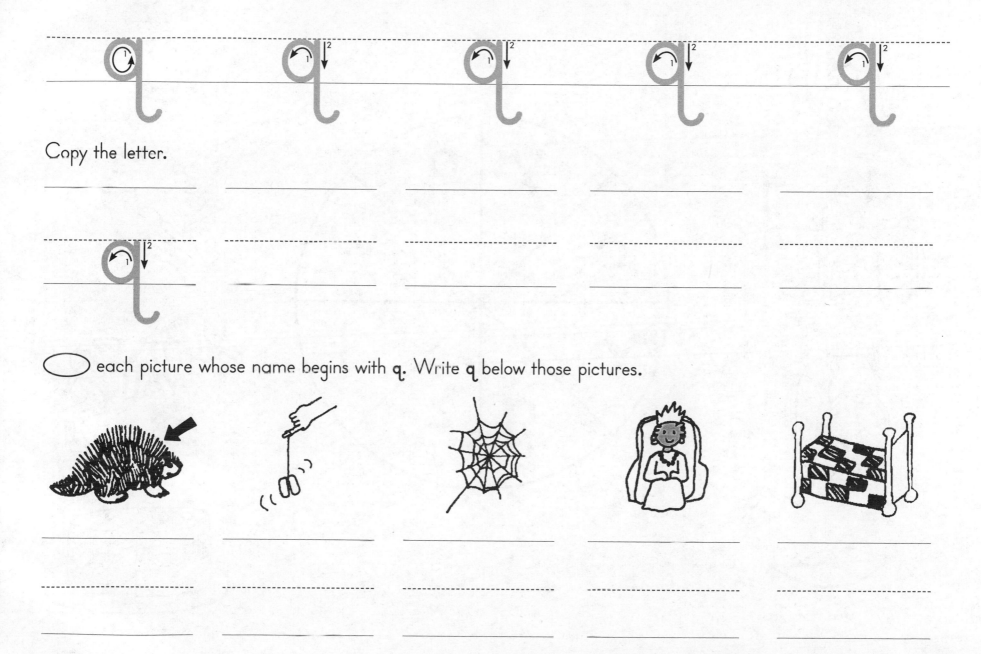

Copy the letter.

each picture whose name begins with **q**. Write **q** below those pictures.

Draw a line from the picture to the letter that begins its name.

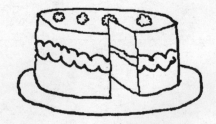

Say the name of the picture and the sound of its first letter.	Find the letter. Circle it.	Write the letter.
	y　z　q　t	
	f　q　v　g	
	v　p　y　w	
	p　t　q　l	
	n　r　v　c	

Draw a line from the picture to the letter that begins its name.

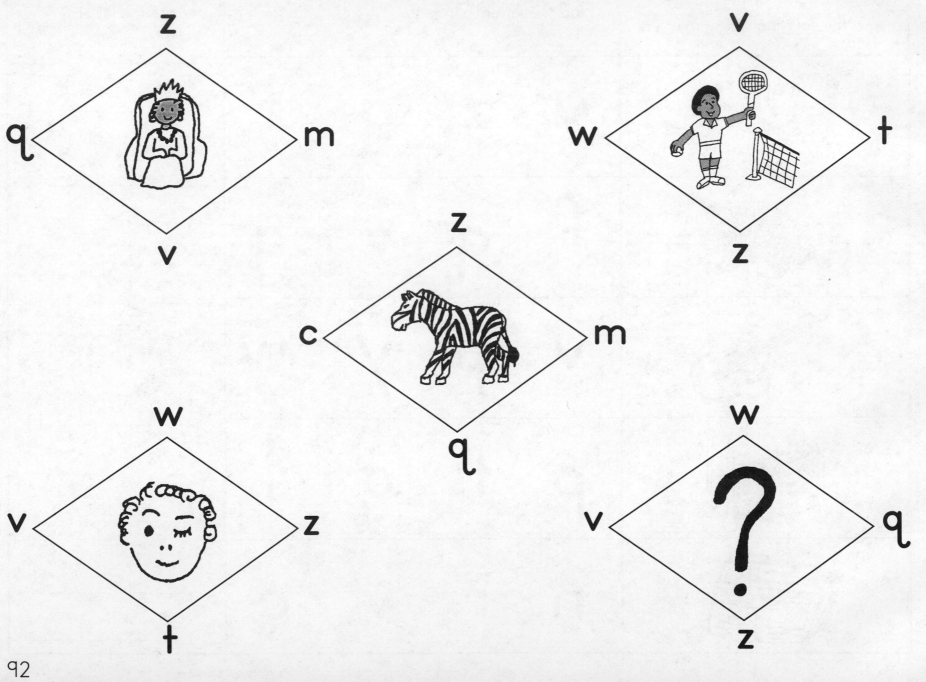

Say the name of the picture and the sound of its first letter.	Find the letter. Circle it.	Write the letter.
	w n z	
	q v w	
	y s v	
	r p z	
	v q m	

Which sound does the word begin with? Write the letter that stands for the sound.

Trace the letter **x** with your finger. This letter has the sound /**ks**/you hear at the **end** of . Say the sound.

Capital letters are used
to begin sentences and names.
A capital **x** looks like this: X.
Capital letters are two spaces tall.

Xx

Teacher: Read the directions aloud while the students listen and work on page 97.

1. This time, listen for the sound that comes at the *end* of a word. *X* sounds like /ks/ and usually is heard at the end of the word. Say the sound the *x* makes. You can hear /ks/ at the end of a word that means a container or a carton. It is used to pack things in. What is it? [box] Put your finger on the **box.** Circle the picture of this word. What sound do you hear at the end of **box?**

2. Now I am thinking of an animal that is the size of a small dog, is red, and has a bushy tail. Say the name of the animal [fox]. Put your finger on the **fox.** Do you hear the /ks/ at the end? Color the **fox** red.

3. When you are cooking or baking, you put things in a bowl and stir. What do we call it when we stir to combine things? [mix] Can you find the picture of **mix?** Put your finger on it. Put a box around the picture. What sound do you hear at the end of **mix?**

4. If something is broken, then we must repair it or have someone _____ it [fix]. Put your finger on the picture of **fix.** What sound do you hear at the end of **fix?** Find the picture of **fix,** and color it any way you like.

5. I am thinking of a number. It is the number of fingers on one hand plus one more finger. How many is that? [six] Put your finger on the **six.** Say the sound you hear at the end of **six.** Draw a fence around the number **six.**

Listen; then follow the directions.

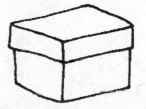

6

Draw a line from each picture to the letter that you hear at the **end** of it.

x   t   g   x   p   k   v

Follow the arrows to write the letter **x**, which says **/ks/** as in 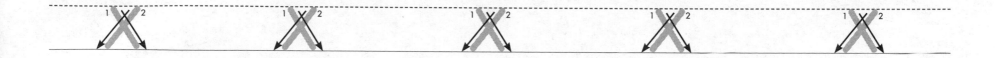. Say the sound aloud.

Copy the letter. Notice that **x** is only one space tall.

each picture whose name **ends** with **x**. Write **x** below those pictures.

Draw a line from the picture to the letter it **ends** with. Remember: Listen for the **last** sound.

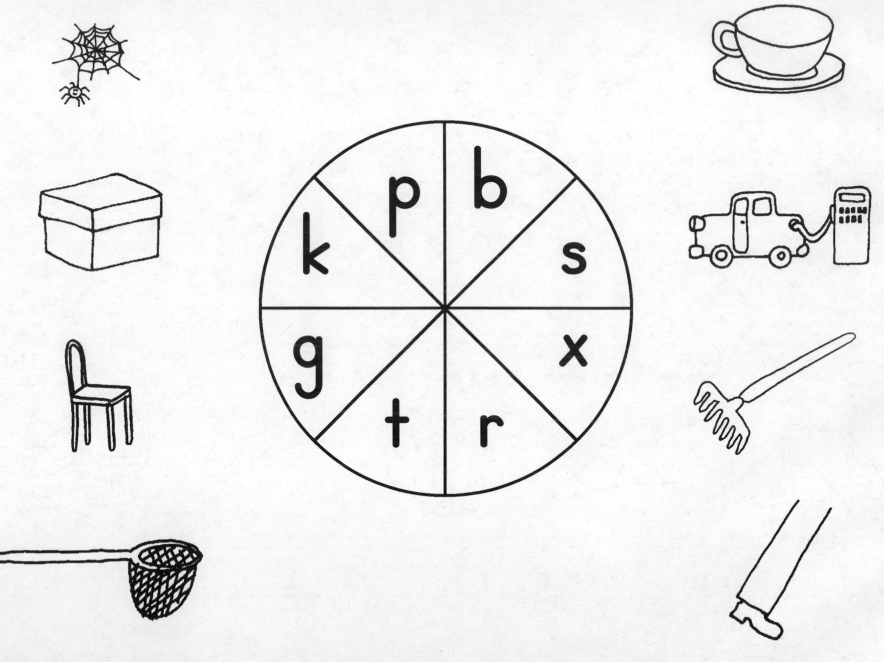

Say the name of the picture and listen to the sound at the **end**.	Find the **ending** letter and circle it.	Write the letter.
	l b f s	
	x k g m	
	d j n x	
	t v z g	
	c f n q	

Which sound does the word **end** with? Circle it. Remember: Listen for the **last** sound.

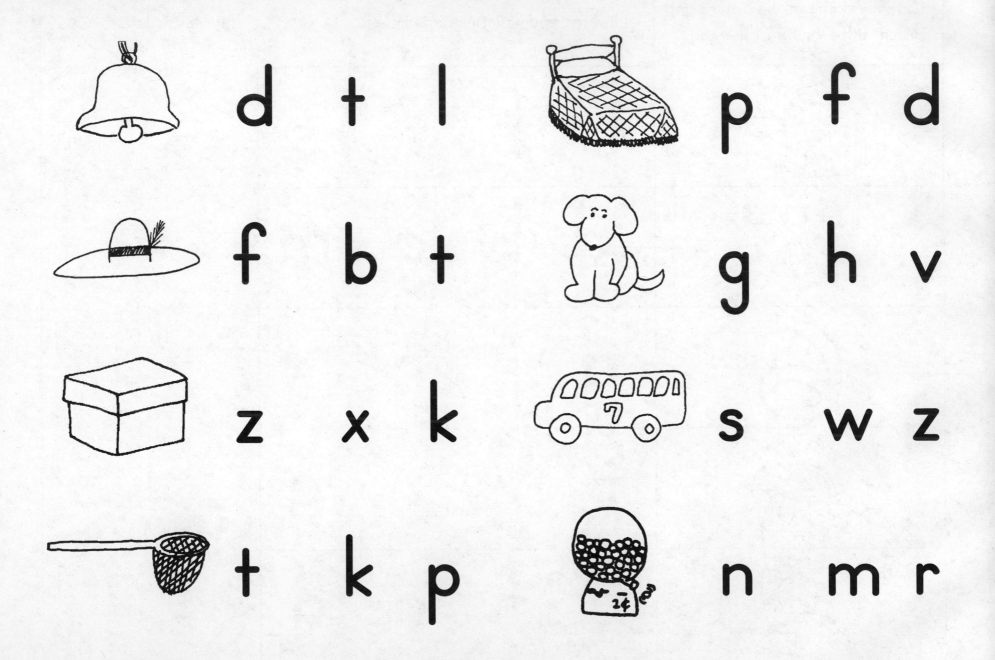

d   t   l

p   f   d

f   b   t

g   h   v

z   x   k

s   w   z

t   k   p

n   m   r

Draw a line from the picture to the letter you hear at the <u>end</u> of the word. Remember: Listen for the <u>last</u> sound.

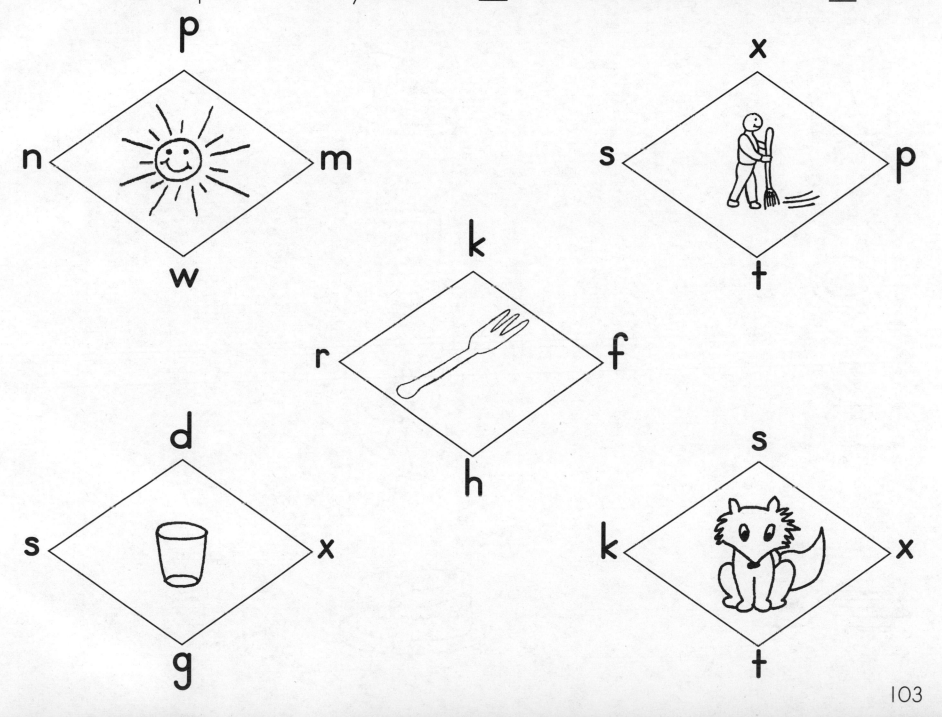

Which sound does the word **end** with? Remember: Listen for the **last** sound. Write the letter that stands for that sound.

Review: Books A, B, C
Which letter does the picture's name **begin** with? Circle it.

v   h   c

m   w   k

d   t   l

m   p   w

r   n   z

f   g   y

s   w   z

b   h   y

Draw a line from the picture to the letter that **begins** its name.

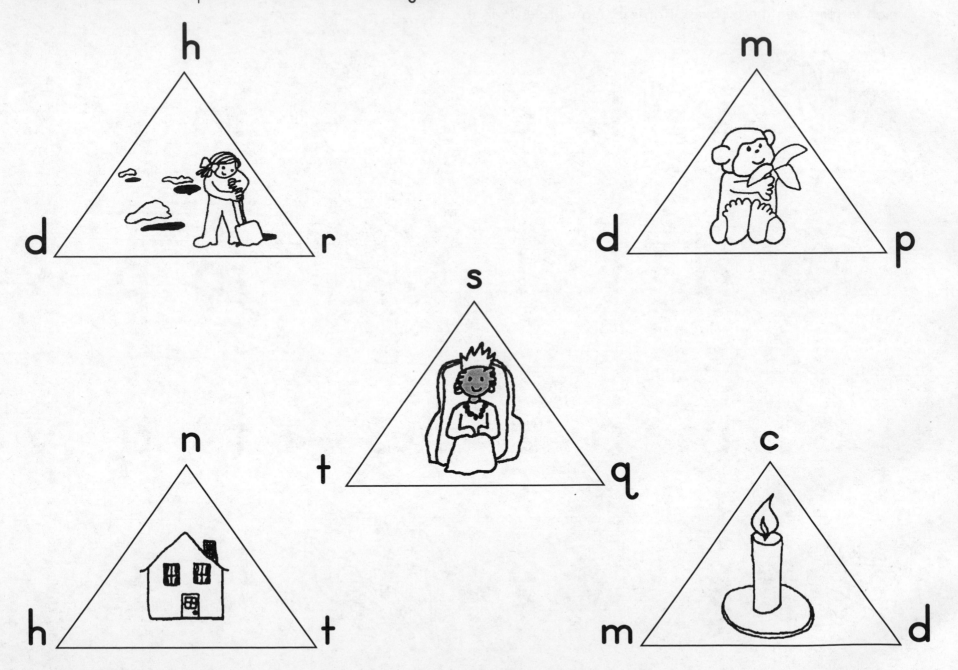

Name the pictures in each row. Which sound do the words **begin** with? Write the letter that stands for that sound.

Draw a line from the picture to the letter that <u>begins</u> its name.

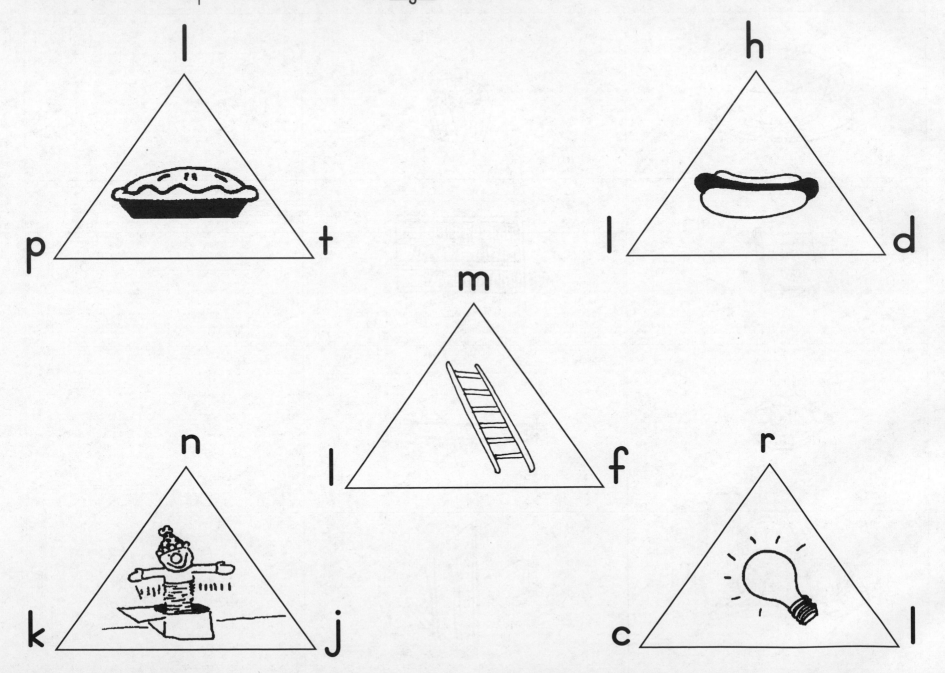

Draw a line from the picture to the letter that <u>begins</u> its name.

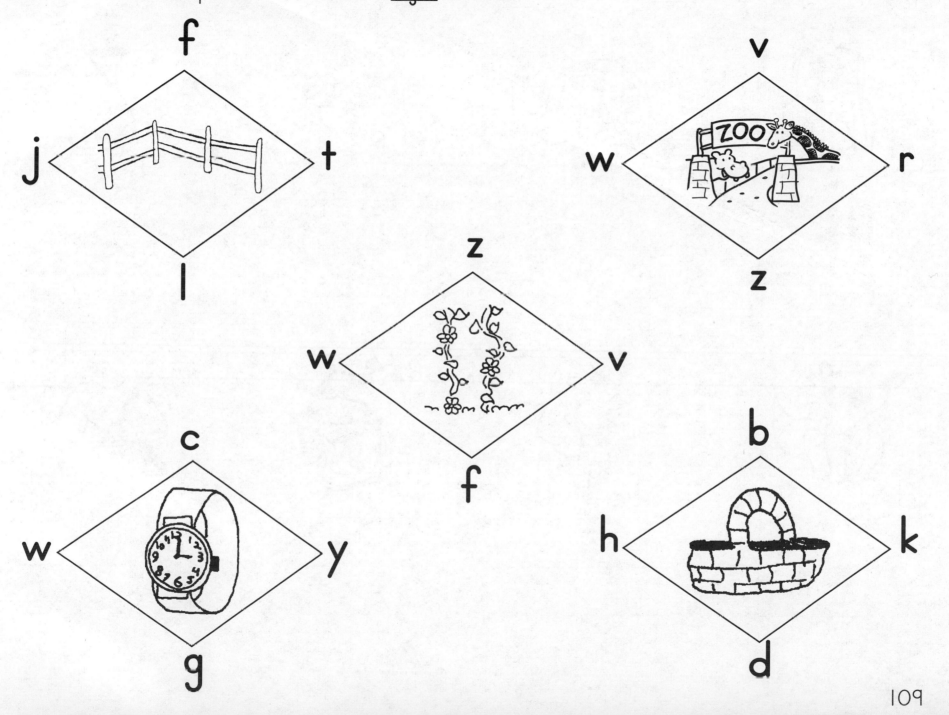

Which sound does the word **begin** with? Write the letter that stands for the sound.